Maryland

Niels R. Jensen

Visit us at
www.abdopublishing.com

Published by ABDO Publishing Company, 8000 West 78th Street, Suite 310, Edina, Minnesota 55439 USA. Copyright ©2010 by Abdo Consulting Group, Inc. International copyrights reserved in all countries. No part of this book may be reproduced in any form without written permission from the publisher. The Checkerboard Library™ is a trademark and logo of ABDO Publishing Company.

Printed in the United States.

Editor: John Hamilton
Graphic Design: Sue Hamilton
Cover Illustration: Neil Klinepier
Cover Photo: iStock Photo
Interior Photo Credits: Alamy, AP Images, Baltimore Orioles, Baltimore Ravens, Comstock, Corbis, Getty, Granger Collection, iStock Photo, Jennifer Boyer, Jimmy Emerson, Library of Congress, Maryland Historical Society Library, Maryland State Archives, Mile High Maps, Mountain High Maps, National Archives, North Wind Picture Archives, and One Mile Up.
Statistics: State population statistics taken from 2008 U.S. Census Bureau estimates. City and town population statistics taken from July 1, 2007, U.S. Census Bureau estimates. Land and water area statistics taken from 2000 Census, U.S. Census Bureau.

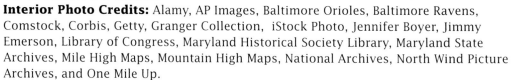

Library of Congress Cataloging-in-Publication Data

Jensen, Niels R., 1949-
  Maryland / Niels Jensen.
      p. cm. -- (The United States)
  Includes index.
  ISBN 978-1-60453-655-3
  1. Maryland--Juvenile literature. I. Title.

  F181.3.J46 2010
  975.2--dc22

                            2008051046

Table of Contents

The Old Line State

Maryland is a state of contrasts. It has sandy beaches and tall mountaintops. It is a border state between the North and South. The culture of rural Maryland resembles the South. But the state's busy cities are like those in the North.

Farming, fishing, and trade made the state wealthy. Manufacturing and high-technology industries followed. The waterways of Chesapeake Bay connect America's roads and railways with the world's markets.

Maryland's nickname is the "Old Line State." It honors the Maryland soldiers who fought bravely during the American Revolution.

The Queen's Landing water tower stands on Kent Island, Maryland.

Name: Maryland is named after Queen Henrietta Maria (1609-1669). She was the wife of England's King Charles I (1600-1649).

State Capital: Annapolis, population 36,603

Date of Statehood: April 28,1788 (7th state)

Population: 5,633,597 (19th-most populous state)

Area (Total Land and Water): 12,407 square miles (32,134 sq km), 42nd-largest state

Largest City: Baltimore, population 637,455

Nickname: Old Line State

Motto: *Fatti Maschii, Parole Femine* (Manly deeds, womanly (gentle) words)

State Bird: Baltimore Oriole

State Flower: Black-Eyed Susan

State Gem: Patuxent River Stone (agate)

State Tree: White Oak

State Song: "Maryland, My Maryland"

Highest Point: Backbone Mountain, 3,360 feet (1,024 m)

Lowest Point: Sea Level (Atlantic Ocean)

Average July Temperature: 75°F (24°C)

Record High Temperature: 109°F (43°C), Cumberland and Frederick, July 10, 1936

Average January Temperature: 33°F (0.5°C)

Record Low Temperature: -40°F (-40°C), Oakland, January 13, 1912

Average Annual Precipitation: 43 inches (109 cm)

Number of U.S. Senators: 2

Number of U.S. Representatives: 8

U.S. Postal Service Abbreviation: MD

Geography

Maryland contains 12,407 square miles (32,134 sq km) of land. It is the 42nd-largest state. It is often called "America in miniature." It has many kinds of land, including sandy beaches, marshlands, and forests.

Glaciers did not cover Maryland during the last ice age, which ended about 14,000 years ago. It is one of the reasons Maryland is the only state that has no natural lakes. Lakes usually form in holes gouged out by glaciers, or where tall glacial deposits surround sections of melting ice.

Maryland's Coastal Plain is the lowland around Chesapeake Bay. It has many creeks, rivers, and marshes. The soil is light and sandy. It is suitable for farming.

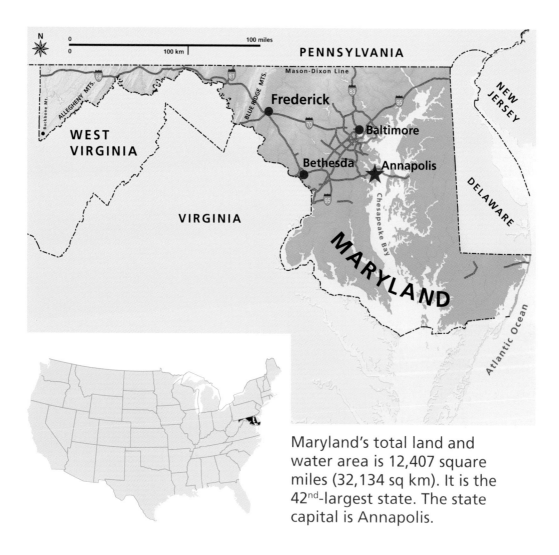

N

0   100 miles
0   100 km

PENNSYLVANIA

Mason-Dixon Line

WEST VIRGINIA

Backbone Mt.

ALLEGHENY MTS.

BLUE RIDGE MTS.

Frederick

Baltimore

Bethesda

Annapolis

VIRGINIA

MARYLAND

Chesapeake Bay

NEW JERSEY

DELAWARE

Atlantic Ocean

Maryland's total land and water area is 12,407 square miles (32,134 sq km). It is the 42nd-largest state. The state capital is Annapolis.

The Piedmont region includes the foothill area of the Appalachian Mountains. It is a region of rolling hills and fertile valleys. There are many dairy farms here.

The Blue Ridge Mountains, Ridge and Valley, and Appalachian Plateau are all part of the Appalachians. The mountainous Blue Ridge area is narrow, less than 20 miles (32 km) wide. The Ridge and Valley region has orchards and farms, but is mostly forests. The Appalachian Plateau has deep valleys that are cut by rivers. It is a forest and mining area.

The Allegheny Mountains are part of the Appalachian Plateau. They include the highest point in Maryland, Backbone Mountain, which rises to 3,360 feet (1,024 m).

Maryland's northern border is the Mason-Dixon Line, which divided the slave states of the South from the free states of the North during the 1800s and the American Civil War.

The Blue Ridge Mountains of Maryland.

Climate and Weather

Maryland's Coastal Plain has a humid climate. The weather is mild, but with some cold winter temperatures.

The state's inland climate has much larger temperature swings. In the western part of Maryland, temperatures can range from well below zero degrees in the winter to more than 100 degrees Fahrenheit (38°C) in the summer.

The state's heaviest rainfalls are in the summer, but they are less regular than in the wintertime. Maryland's driest area is the Ridge and Valley region. Mountains to the west and east shield it from rain and snow. In Maryland's western mountains, however, there can often be heavy snowfalls. The state's average annual precipitation is 43 inches (109 cm).

Naval Academy cadets in Annapolis, Maryland, go for a morning jog despite heavy rain and high winds.

Plants and Animals

Maryland has about 2.5 million acres (1 million ha) of woodlands, almost half of the state's land surface. There are 5 state forests and 65 state parks. National parks include the Assateague Island National Seashore and Catoctin Mountain Park. A 40-mile (64-km) section of the Appalachian Trail goes through the state.

Maryland has more than 160 kinds of trees. Oak and hickory make up 60 percent of forested areas. Loblolly pine is common along Maryland's eastern shore.

Many white-tailed and sika deer roam Maryland's forests. The state also has bobcat, coyote, chipmunk, fisher, fox, black bear, mink, muskrat, opossum, otter, skunk, and squirrel. The famous wild Chincoteague horses live on Assateague Island.

Wild Chincoteague horses live on Assateague Island.

Sika Deer

Fisher

Fox

Maryland's game birds include duck, grouse, pheasant, quail, and turkey. The Delmarva Peninsula's marshes and wildlife refuges have eagles, herons, geese, osprey, and swans. Other birds include bluebirds, cardinals, doves, hawks, hummingbirds, owls, and robins.

There are 27 species of snakes in the state. Only two are poisonous, the copperhead and timber rattlesnake.

Maryland's inland and ocean waters have many fish. They include bass, bluegill, carp, catfish, flounder, herring, marlin, pike, shad, shark, trout, tuna, and walleye. Many shellfish are harvested in Chesapeake Bay. They include blue crab, clams, oysters, and scallops.

A blue crab.

Whales are often spotted off the Atlantic coast. These include humpback, blue, minke, and other whales. There are also porpoises and sea turtles in the state's waters.

A great blue heron in Maryland's Blackwater National Wildlife Refuge.

History

There were people in the Maryland area about 12,000 years ago. By about 2,000 BC, these Native Americans grew corn, peas, squash, and tobacco. Hunting and fishing were also important.

English explorer John Smith sailed into the Chesapeake Bay area in 1608. In 1632, King Charles I of England gave permission to start a colony. Leonard Calvert was the colony's first governor. The colony was named Maryland in honor of the king's wife, Queen Henrietta Maria.

Maryland made money by raising tobacco, which was the colony's main cash crop. Servants, convicts, and African slaves were brought in to harvest the crop.

In 1694, the assembly moved the colony's capital to Annapolis. It was a rich city, partly because of its port.

John Smith explored the Chesapeake Bay area in 1608.

Maryland's northern border became known as the Mason-Dixon Line. It divided the slave states from the free states during the 1800s until the Civil War.

The people of Maryland joined the American

From 1763 to 1767, Charles Mason and Jeremiah Dixon surveyed the boundary line between Maryland and Pennsylvania. This became known as the Mason-Dixon Line.

Revolution in 1775. There were no battles in the state, but soldiers from Maryland fought bravely in the war. Maryland ratified the United States Constitution on April 28, 1788. It also later gave land for Washington, D.C., the nation's new capital.

The British attacked Baltimore's Fort McHenry during the War of 1812, but could not destroy it. The national anthem of the United States, "The Star-Spangled Banner," was written about the event. After the war, commerce, industry, and transportation grew.

In September 1814, Francis Scott Key was held on a British ship in Baltimore Harbor. He saw the bombing of Fort McHenry and the American flag. It inspired Key to write "The Star-Spangled Banner."

The Civil War began in 1861. Maryland stayed in the United States, even though other slave states joined the Confederacy. Maryland's people fought on both sides of the war, but most served in the Union army. There were battles in Maryland, including the Battle of Antietam in 1862. It was the bloodiest day of battle in the war. More than 23,000 soldiers were killed or wounded. Before the Civil War ended in 1865, Maryland's state constitution was rewritten to end slavery.

One of the bloodiest battles of the Civil War happened in September 1862 in northwestern Maryland, near Antietam Creek. It is known as the Battle of Antietam.

Maryland continued to develop as an American crossroads. More railroads and highways were built. Baltimore grew as a major port and industrial center. It became very important during World War I (1914-1918) and World War II (1939-1945). People also moved into the areas near Washington, D.C., forming large suburbs. It's a growth that continues to this day.

During World War II, the Baltimore plant of the Glenn L. Martin Company built B-26 Marauder bombers.

Did You Know?

- In 1781, Maryland's John Hanson (1721–1783) became the first president of Congress under the new nation's Articles of Confederation. This was before the United States became official. George Washington became the first president after the U.S. Constitution was ratified in 1789.

- Jousting is Maryland's official sport. Competitions can be seen from May through October, and at the Maryland Renaissance Festival.

- The anti-slavery book *Uncle Tom's Cabin,* by Harriet Beecher Stowe, became a best seller in the mid-1800s. The cabin of Josiah Henson, who was the inspiration for Tom, is still standing in Rockville, Maryland.

- Construction of a national road from Cumberland to the Ohio River Valley was approved in 1806. It was the first interstate highway.

- Washington, D.C., was carved out of Maryland in 1790. Virginia contributed another section, but it was returned in 1847.

People

Frederick Douglass (1818-1895) was born a slave in Maryland. He escaped and became an abolitionist speaker, author, and newspaper publisher. After the Civil War, he worked hard for civil rights for all people. He was an advisor to United States presidents, and held several government jobs.

Jim Henson (1936-1990) was a puppeteer and film producer who grew up and went to college in Maryland. He created *The Muppets* and worked on *Sesame Street*. Kermit the Frog, Miss Piggy, Big Bird, and Cookie Monster are among the many beloved characters he helped develop.

Francis Scott Key (1779-1843) watched the 25-hour attack on Baltimore's Fort McHenry during the War of 1812. After the attack, the American flag was still flying over the fort. Key was inspired to write "The Star-Spangled Banner," which became America's national anthem. Key was born in Carroll County, Maryland.

Thurgood Marshall (1908-1993) became the first African American United States Supreme Court justice in 1967. Earlier, he had argued before the Court that having separate public schools for African American and white children was unconstitutional. The Court agreed. Marshall was born in Baltimore, Maryland.

George Herman "Babe" Ruth, Jr.
(1895-1948) was one of baseball's greatest players. He was only 19 when a baseball scout signed the teen to play for the Baltimore Orioles. He is most famous as a power-hitter for the New York Yankees, from 1920-1925. Ruth had a lifetime record of 714 home runs. He was born in Baltimore.

Edgar Allan Poe (1809-1849) wrote stories and poems of mystery and horror, including "The Raven" and *The Pit and the Pendulum*. He is also one of the inventors of detective stories. He is buried in Baltimore.

Harriet Tubman (1820?-1913) was born into slavery in Maryland, but escaped. She became a major leader in the Underground Railroad. Over the course of 10 years, she went back to the South 19 times to help more than 300 other slaves escape to freedom. She also worked as a cook, a nurse, and even a Union spy during the Civil War.

Michael Phelps (1985-) is a record-winning swimmer who was born in Baltimore. At 15, he competed in his first Olympics. In 2008, he won eight gold medals at the Summer Olympic Games in Beijing, China. He has 14 gold medals, plus two bronze medals.

Cities

A marina in Annapolis.

Annapolis became the capital of Maryland in 1694. Its population is 36,603. It served as the capital of the United States from 1783 to 1784. The city today still has many buildings from the 1600s and 1700s. It is a popular place for tourists to visit. It was once a port for the slave trade. Today, Annapolis is regarded as a major center for boating and sailing in America. It is the home of the United States Naval Academy.

Baltimore is a busy seaport. It is Maryland's largest city, with a population of 637,455. There are several major financial businesses located there. Baltimore's largest employers are Johns Hopkins University and Johns Hopkins Hospital. In the 1800s, Baltimore was one of the main entry ports for European immigrants.

Bethesda is a Maryland suburb of Washington, D.C. It has a population of 55,277. It is the home of the National Institutes of Health, Consumer Product Safety Commission, Bethesda Naval Hospital, Lockheed Martin, and Marriott International.

The National Naval Medical Center in Bethesda, Maryland.

Frederick grew around a crossroad. Both Union and Confederate troops marched through the area during the Civil War. Today, the city has a population of 59,220. It is home to a large factory that makes solar panels. The United States Army's Fort Detrick is also located in Frederick. It employs many people. Researchers there work in biology and medicine.

Frederick has been a crossroad city since the late 1800s. Today, it is located at the junction of Interstate I-70, Interstate I-270, U.S. Route 340, U.S. Route 40 and U.S. Route 15.

Transportation

Baltimore's deep-water harbor is important for shipping freight. It supports approximately 23,000 jobs in the area. It also has docks and services used by cruise ships.

Baltimore's Inner Harbor.

There are several railways providing freight services in Maryland. The largest are CSX and Norfolk Southern. There are also many passenger trains in the state. Baltimore Penn Station is one of the nation's busiest rail passenger terminals.

The Chesapeake Bay Bridge is one of the world's longest bridges. It connects Maryland's Eastern and Western Shore regions.

Maryland's largest airport is the Baltimore/Washington International Thurgood Marshall Airport. Nearly 21 million passengers use it every year.

Maryland's Interstate highways include I-68, I-70, I-81, I-83, I-95, I-97. There are 2,584 bridges in the state. The 4.3-mile (6.9-km) Chesapeake Bay Bridge is one of world's longest bridges. About 26 million trucks and cars use it each year.

Natural Resources

Maryland's agriculture industry is ranked 36th in the nation. It employs about 63,000 people, and has $1.8 billion in sales. Products include chickens, greenhouse and nursery crops, grains, soybeans, dairy, organic foods, wine, and tobacco. The average farm size is 160 acres (65 ha).

A dairy farm in Westminster, Maryland.

Commercial fishing is important in Maryland. Chesapeake Bay's blue crab is world famous. Oysters, clams, and fish are also harvested. Some of Chesapeake Bay's traditional skipjack boats

A skipjack is also known as an oyster dredge boat. Only a few are still used for fishing.

are still left, but only a few are used for fishing.

The state's timber and wood products create $2.2 billion in sales, and employ 14,000 workers. Related industries include sawmilling, paper manufacturing, cabinet making, and furniture making.

Western Maryland has several active coal mines. Approximately 5 million tons (4.5 million metric tons) of coal is mined each year.

Industry

  Maryland is one of the nation's wealthiest states. It is home to many important high technology, software, aerospace, and defense businesses. Finance and insurance companies also do business in the state. Because employment is so good, Maryland is the fourth-largest retail market in the United States. Retail stores sell about $95 billion in goods each year in the state.

  Maryland is a national center for the health and life sciences. It has many well-known hospitals and research centers. These include Johns Hopkins Hospital, Bethesda Naval Hospital, the University of Maryland, and the National Institutes of Health.

Manufacturing is still a part of Maryland's economy. Steel, aluminum, chemicals, machinery, and car parts are made here. There are also printing and publishing companies.

Tourism is very important to Maryland. About 28 million people visit the state each year. They create $11 billion in business, employing about 116,000 people.

Johns Hopkins Hospital in Baltimore is a world-famous medical center.

Sports

Maryland's professional sports teams include the National Football League's Baltimore Ravens and Major League Baseball's Baltimore Orioles.

The U.S. Naval Academy at Annapolis has a football rivalry with the U.S. Military Academy at West Point, New York. Army-Navy games get national attention.

Maryland is a great place to enjoy the outdoors. Bird watching, backpacking, bicycling, camping, golfing, hiking, running, and skiing are popular pastimes.

People come to swim and surf along the Atlantic coastline. There is parasailing, kayaking, canoeing, and windsurfing on the ocean and inland waters.

Chesapeake Bay is world famous for boating and sailing. Maryland also has fine freshwater and saltwater fishing.

The state's big-game hunting includes black bear and white-tail deer. People also hunt turkey, quail, pheasant, grouse, duck, and Canada goose.

An early-morning rower.

Entertainment

The Baltimore Museum of Art has more than 90,000 items in its collection. It includes works from such painters as Vincent van Gogh, Pablo Picasso, and Andy Warhol. The Walters Art Museum is also in Baltimore.

Other Maryland museums include the Chesapeake Bay Maritime Museum, the Maryland Science Center, the National Museum of Civil War Medicine, and the United States Naval Academy Museum. The Baltimore & Ohio Railroad Museum has one of the finest collections of steam locomotives from the 1800s.

There are professional symphony orchestras in Annapolis, Baltimore, Bethesda, and Hagerstown, and an opera company in Baltimore.

Maryland has four tracks for horse racing, and two harness tracks. The state fair is held in Timonium.

There are several amusement parks in Ocean City, and Six Flags America is in Mitchellville. Other attractions include Baltimore's Maryland Zoo, the National Aquarium, as well as Salisbury's Zoological Park.

Visitors enjoy the beach and the attractions in Ocean City, Maryland.

Timeline

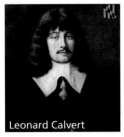

Leonard Calvert

1632—England's King Charles I grants permission to start a colony. Leonard Calvert is the colony's first governor.

1788—Maryland becomes the seventh state.

1814—During the War of 1812, British fire on Fort McHenry. Seeing this, Francis Scott Key writes "The Star-Spangled Banner."

1844—World's first telegraph connects Washington, D.C., and Baltimore.

1845—U.S. Naval Academy is established in Annapolis.

1861—The Civil War begins. Maryland stays in the Union.

1862—Confederate forces are stopped at the Battle of Antietam.

1864—Maryland ends slavery.

1873—Johns Hopkins Hospital and University founded.

1952—Chesapeake Bay Bridge is completed.

2008—Swimmer Michael Phelps, a Maryland native, wins a record eight gold medals at the 2008 Summer Olympic Games in Beijing, China.

Glossary

Abolitionist—A person who favors the banning of an activity, such as slavery, or the death penalty.

Articles of Confederation—The written rules for the first United States government. It was approved by the original 13 states in 1781. The Articles of Confederation were replaced by the U.S. Constitution in 1789.

Confederacy—A group of 11 Southern states that broke away from the United States during the Civil War, which lasted from 1861 until 1865.

Delmarva Peninsula—The Delmarva Peninsula lies between the Atlantic Ocean, Chesapeake Bay, and Delaware Bay. Its name is short for (Del)aware, (Mar)yland, and (V)irgini(a). All three states have a part of it.

Ice Age—An ice age happens when Earth's climate causes a major growth of the polar ice caps, continental ice shelves, and glaciers. The ice sheets can be more than one mile (1.6 km) thick.

Interstate—Existing or carried between states. A busy road that crosses state lines is called an interstate highway.

Mason-Dixon Line—The Mason-Dixon Line is Maryland's northern border. It separates the northern and southern regions of the U.S. The states south of the line were slave states.

Ratify—To sign or approve a document, such as a treaty or contract, to make it official.

Suburb—The outer parts of a major city, especially where large numbers of people live. Many suburbs are cities themselves.

Underground Railroad—The Underground Railroad helped African Americans escape from the slave states. It wasn't a real railroad. Instead, it was a secret network of safe houses and connecting routes that led people to freedom.

Index

APR 2010